The Teacher's Space

Weekly ideas for creating a teacher workspace that uplifts your spirit

BY TALIA MILLER

DEDICATION

To all of the educators who are managing classroom set-up

As we work to create wonderful learning spaces for our students, this is to remind us to carve out our own joyful workspaces that will lift our spirits on a daily basis!

Copyright © 2024 Talia Miller
All rights reserved.
ISBN: 9798852179920
Independently published

CONTENTS

The Idea………………………………………	4
The Snack Drawer…………………………..	6
The Zip Pouch………………………………	8
The Cords……………………………………	10
The Colors…………………………………..	12
The Leafy Plant……………………………	14
The Succulent………………………………	16
The Sound…………………………………..	18
The Scent……………………………………	20
The Real Utensils…………………………	22
The Webcam………………………………	24
The Art………………………………………	26
The Quote Space…………………………	28
The Lamp…………………………………..	30
The Walk……………………………………	32
The Vase……………………………………	34
The Bowl……………………………………	36
The Screensaver…………………………	38
The Organizer……………………………	40
The Tools……………………………………	42
The Temperature…………………………	44
The Cushion………………………………..	46
The Idea Space……………………………	48
The Two Photos…………………………..	50
The Figurine………………………………	52
The Joy Box………………………………..	54
Conclusion…………………………………	56

Intro Connectivity

As teachers, we work hard to set up our classroom spaces to optimize learning and, importantly, to help students build connections. We hope not only that they connect with the content, but also that they connect with each other. Online and through observation, we can find an abundance of ideas for classroom organization, furniture placement, set up of stations and materials, and general decoration. The work that we do and the choices that we make help our students find community and engagement in our classrooms. With a holistic lens, our classroom design choices are made with a student-centered focus. This book is about engaging in a small amount of design work specifically for ourselves. Within that space that is student-focused, we need an anchoring workspace that is designed to nurture our own, specific needs. In your classroom, how can you create a teacher's space?

OPTIONS

- The book is set up to explore one idea per week.
- You can change the timing or order, but the order was chosen with a sequencing in mind.
- Each idea can be modified - you can go basic or upgrade - the joy in this is making it your own.

MAKE IT HAPPEN

- You will likely have some of these ideas in place, but take time to rework what you have so that it becomes even more intentional and authentic.
- You may be a room-floating teacher. Your effort could become more focused on your desk and desk area, wherever that is located.
- You may share a room with an assistant, and you can coordinate, or even better, actually each individually develop your own teacher's space.
- The space will inherently overlap with the space of the students, but the difference is to choose a piece of art, etc, specifically for you.

Remember: you can work on your room all you like, but this design work is to be done through the lens of creating an intentionally nurturing teacher's space

Week 1
The Snack Drawer

The goal of our first week will be to create a teacher-focused snack drawer. As a busy teacher, your snacks and drinks need to be readily available in a central location. Snacks help us maintain our energy and curb hunger between meals. They can provide important nutrients, and they help us create healthy eating routines.

OPTIONS

- An actual drawer
- A basket in a drawer or in a cabinet
- A box that you keep with you on your cart

ITEMS YOU CAN GATHER

- Mug or cup for drinks
- Tea, hot chocolate, coffee pods
- Water bottle that you can keep in snack drawer or on your desk if preferred
- Dry snacks such as almonds, crackers, pretzels
- Fruits (fresh or dried)
- Granola, cereal, or protein bars
- Chocolate treat
- Mints or hard candy treat

MAKE IT HAPPEN

- You could consider getting dividers or small containers to go in the drawer.
- You could decide how often you want to stock it, and fill it accordingly. You might bring fruit or veggies on a more daily basis, or stock dry snacks on Mondays.
- You could easily keep a bag of pretzels with a clip, and have a small, fun bowl that you use when you are ready to snack.
- It may be nice to have some napkins in the drawer.

Remember: you may have a stash of granola bars for students somewhere else, but this is to be your space - the teacher's space

Week 2
The Zip Pouch

The goal of our our second week will be to create a zip pouch with items that you may need for taking care of yourself. At times, you may find yourself with a headache or cough, or you may need something more basic like a safety pin or deodorant refresh. Your zip pouch will have things to help get you through your day and to help you feel ready and prepared for these unexpected needs.

OPTIONS

- Toiletry pouch
- Cosmetic bag
- Small gear bag

ITEMS YOU CAN GATHER

- Aspirin/ibuprofen, cough drops
- Extra reading glasses
- Nail clippers, nail file, tweezers
- Dental floss, toothpicks, toothbrush
- Deodorant
- Lip balm, chapstick
- Menstrual hygiene products
- Instant stain remover stick
- Comb, hairbrush, hair ties, headband
- Safety pins

MAKE IT HAPPEN

- You could use any type of zip pouch, or even a small handled bag. But it should be a bag you can grab and easily take to the bathroom if needed.
- Any pouch can help you keep needed items together, but having a closure helps provide you some privacy.
- You might additionally add some band aids or your own first aid items, if you don't have a general classroom stash of those already.

Remember: the bag should bring you joy, so choose something that is outdoorsy, floral, plain canvas, or other - whatever materials will help you feel happy to grab it when you need it

Week 3
The Cords

Our goal this week is power cord and device charger organization. Tidiness and easy access to device chargers will help your workspace feel welcoming and efficient. Getting the cords dusted and situated will reduce cord frustration. Creating an organized space that provides for your power cord needs will help your space feel supportive and more personalized.

OPTIONS

- For power cords, you can use ties to organize, or you may need a power strip to centralize.
- For charging, you may need additional cords, a charging station, or a charging pad.

ITEMS YOU CAN GATHER

- Dusting materials
- Cable ties, twist ties, velcro straps
- Any additional charging cords or power strips
- Other types of cord organizers or charging stations, depending on your needs
- Command strips

MAKE IT HAPPEN

- Stretch out and dust all current power cords. Determine where you would like the coiled cord to sit or hang, and use a tie to secure.
- Obtain any extra needed gear for charging your devices. Maybe you'd like a charging pad for your phone, but need a station or table organizer for your charging cords.
- You can use command strips to attach hooks to your desk, or you can use the strips to anchor down organizers. Take your time to put together a good system for yourself.

While you work: check to see that your cords are in good condition and properly secured - the goal is that they are neatly as well as safely out your way

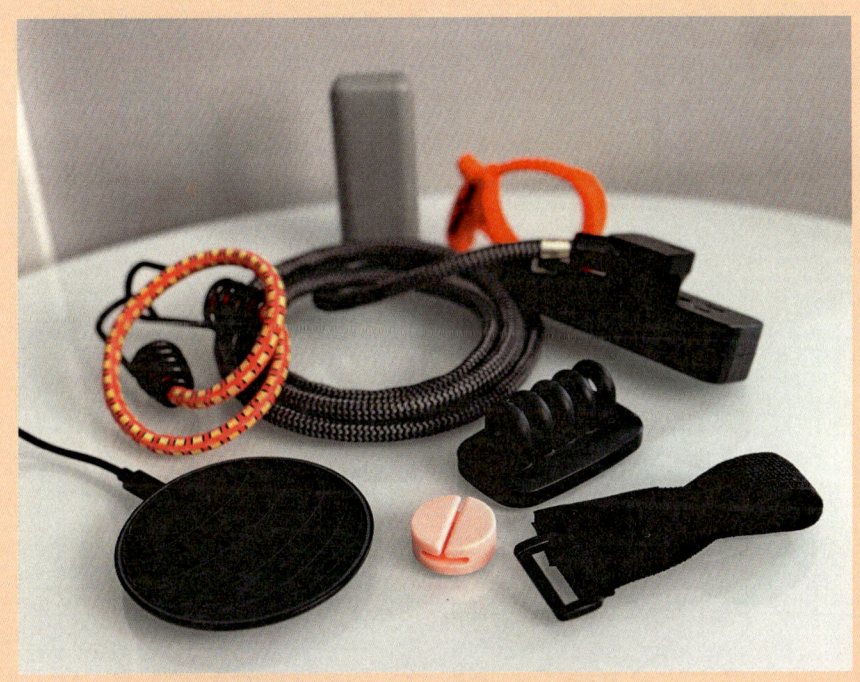

Week 4
The Colors

This week we will focus on a thematic color palette. Your room already has decorative color, but you will choose two colors that will connect and ground you in your workspace. Color has the ability to influence your mood, and your associations with color will impact how you feel. By choosing two colors that you have a positive connection with, you can further personalize your space to support your well being.

OPTIONS

- Look online for colors and their meanings, and choose two that match your vibe.
- Look at colors in your photos, especially outdoor ones, or take a walk in your neighborhood and see which colors you notice.
- Think about memories that you associate with particular colors, such swimming at a beach, watching a sunset, or hiking in a forest.
- Decide on a couple of colors that you really like, and acquire a few productivity items in these colors.

ITEMS YOU CAN GATHER

- Pens, pencils, markers
- Post-it notes, a notepad, paper or binder clips
- Stapler, hole punch, pencil cup, ruler
- Trays, baskets, organizer

MAKE IT HAPPEN

- You may already have some items in the color that you choose. Gather them on your desk in an organizer, or cluster them in your desk drawer to see them when you open it.
- Consider purchasing post-it notes. You could put a new one each day on your desk with 2-3 things you need to remember for that day.
- If you have patterned thick paper in your colors, make a bookmark with it to use with textbooks.
- Experiment with colored file folders, file folder labels, or paper clips, or purchase yourself a new pen to try out in a color that you like.

Going forward: as you make additions to your workspace, keep your color choices in mind to bring cohesiveness to your space

Week 5
The Leafy Plant

Our goal this week will be to add a leafy plant to your workspace. Plants can bring joy and connection to nature into your life. They can help you feel calm, content, and focused. Plants add green to your space, give you something to nurture, and provide health benefits.

OPTIONS

- The plant could be placed on your desk, shelf, window sill, stand or the floor, or could even hang.
- Resilient plants include spider plants, dracaena, pothos, philodendron, and parlor palms.

ITEMS YOU CAN GATHER

- Plant
- Pot/container for the plant, tray
- Small bag of potting soil
- Refillable water bottle or watering can to water the plant
- Fertilizer appropriate for the plant
- Plant stand
- Wall bracket and hanging pot
- A cloth to dust the leaves

MAKE IT HAPPEN

- When choosing a plant, be mindful of the amount of light and frequency of watering.
- Consider starting with a size that could be watered with your refillable water bottle to make it easier to maintain.
- Choose a container for the plant that matches the color choices you like to see in your space.
- Purchase fertilizer and make note of care needs when you purchase the plant.

Remember: choose something considered fairly low maintenance so that you are able to keep it alive easily

Week 6
The Succulent

This week, our goal is to add a succulent plant as a partner to last week's leafy plant. The succulent and its container will serve as a contrasting companion to the leafy plant and its container. The plant leaves of each should be different and complement each other, and the plant pots should be harmonious with each other. The pairing will serve as a natural, green oasis in your workspace.

OPTIONS

- The succulent can be placed next to the leafy plant at the same level or on a small shelf, or possibly suspended nearby.
- Resilient plants include jade, aloe vera, haworthia zebra, donkey tail, and paddle plant.

ITEMS YOU CAN GATHER

- Plant that structurally contrasts with your leafy plant (lobed, smooth, spined, etc)
- Container that is a decorative companion with your leafy plant container (such as one smooth and one textured, or one plain and one patterned)
- Other materials similar to last week

MAKE IT HAPPEN

- View the new succulent as a companion to your leafy plant.
- Choose not only a plant and container that you like, but again, one that goes with the leafy plant.
- Think about the two or so colors that you have chosen for decorating, and see if you can work within that color scheme to keep your space cohesive.

Remember: these plants are to be partners - add the succulent to create the grouping

Week 7
The Sound

The goal this week is to incorporate uplifting sound into your space during your preparation times. As teachers, our days are filled with dialogue, large discussions, and sometimes even verbal conflict. Music and other relaxing types of sounds can enhance your health and well being. The sounds can reduce anxiety, improve your mood and/or productivity, and serve to help you relax.

OPTIONS

- Local radio station
- Music playlist
- Podcast
- Sporting event
- Website or app that offers background noise such as coffee shop, library, nature, rain, etc.

ITEMS YOU CAN GATHER

- Radio
- Phone or computer
- Earphones, headphones, or speaker
- Playlist
- Online videos or broadcasts with chosen content

MAKE IT HAPPEN

- You can get a radio that streams, leaving yourself options.
- You could make a desk work playlist for grading, as well as a livelier clean-your-room playlist for a speaker.
- Numerous fun background noises are available such as crackling fire, chimes, frogs, and autumn breezes, and some sites will even let you combine noises such as wind, rustling leaves, and a crackling fire.

Remember: you will be doing different types of tasks during your preparation time, so outfit yourself with a few options to create a great space to work

Week 8
The Scent

The goal of this week is to find a couple of ways that you can bring a wonderful scent into your workspace. Our classroom spaces can take on a closed-building smell at times, and it is nice to add a subtle aromatic. Scents can increase alertness or create feelings of calm. Scents have been shown to promote mental health and wellbeing, and the scents you choose can connect you with your memories or help your space feel more personalized.

OPTIONS

- Plant-based items
- Burnable items
- Diffusers or air fresheners
- Self-care products that you use that carry a scent

ITEMS YOU CAN GATHER

- Flowers, plants, essential oil diffusers
- Candles or incense, matches
- Lotion, chapstick or other personal care items
- Natural or fresh-smelling cleaners
- Nicely-scented soaps

MAKE IT HAPPEN

- Bouquets or pine branches can bring fragrance to a space and can also be seasonal in nature.
- Burning a candle during your preparation time allows you to enjoy the smell, and it will likely linger only a bit after being blown out.
- Essential oils can be combined in different ways, and be used in lower concentration so the scent is subtle.
- A great soap or hand lotion can add a temporary scent that brings freshness to your day.

Remember: you are adding the scent for you, and it should be present in a subtle way, but not overwhelming to students when they are in space that overlaps with yours

Week 9
The Real Utensils

This week's goal is to add real utensils to your workspace collection. When eating lunch or snacks, it is convenient to have a fork, spoon, and knife, a bowl and/or plate, and a mug. These can be real utensils, such as a beautiful metal fork or a colorful ceramic mug, rather than disposable or plastic items. Utensils come in contact with your food and even your mouth, and having beautiful ones will help you enjoy your lunch or snack experience.

OPTIONS

- Ceramic, stoneware
- Glass
- Metal or enameled
- Wood

ITEMS YOU CAN GATHER

- Stoneware or ceramic mug for hot items such as tea or coffee
- Glass for water or packet drinks like Emergen-C
- Metal straw
- Ceramic plate or bowl
- Metal or wooden silverware

MAKE IT HAPPEN

- You likely have some of these items, but consider a switch out to have fun, beautiful versions, perhaps coordinating with the colors you have chosen for yourself.
- You could consider adding a cloth component such as a napkin or placemat.
- Think about finding utensils to help your eating experience feel civilized, rather than hurried for frenetic.

Remember: eating to fuel your body is an important part of your day, and having utensils that bring joy will help you feel relaxed when you take a break to have the food you need to sustain yourself

Week 10
The Webcam

Your goal this week will be to explore having a webcam on during your preparation time. As we work in our classrooms, it can be a wonderful experience to connect with the world. Live webcam streams are available to see scenic areas, special landmarks, and tourist locations, as well as nature and wildlife.

OPTIONS

- Computer screen webcam
- Projection of webcam in your room

CONSIDER EXPLORING

- Your favorite beach or mountain
- Vacation spots
- Cities
- Nesting birds
- Aquariums
- National parks (Old Faithful)
- Specialty sites (Abbey Road)
- African wildlife
- Animal cams (service dog training)
- Northern lights
- International space station

MAKE IT HAPPEN

- There is a webcam available to suit any interests, so spend some time doing a little web research to find some that you like.
- Bookmark a few, as they can vary based on the time of day.
- Strive to find actual, live webcams, as it helps connect you with something going on, at that very moment, somewhere else in the world.

Remember: as you do preparation work during a planning period, the webcam can offer a window into the world, and often may bring a smile, depending on what you choose

Week 11
The Art

Our focus this week is on adding a piece of art to your workspace. While visually decorative, art can also speak to our souls. Art has the ability to reduce anxiety and elevate your mood. It can be an anchor point to increase your sense of connection and contentment.

OPTIONS

- Poster or photography print
- Painting
- Collage
- Tapestry

IDEAS TO CONSIDER

- Use an enlargement of a photo of a vacation spot with scenery or botanicals.
- Use a poster or painting purchased locally or online.
- Hang a small tapestry or woven piece of art.
- Explore displaying a photo with or without a mat.
- You will need to get hanging materials, such as command strips, or mount a small shelf on which to place your art.

MAKE IT HAPPEN

- It would be ideal to have the art hanging right by your workspace.
- If you purchase a standard-sized frame, you could easily change out a photo for variety.
- You could consider a cluster of photos, such as three in a row, with similar subject matter.
- Make choices that feel personal, yet professional, such as a beach you love, but maybe not you in your swimsuit at that beach.

Remember: art has the ability to touch your heart and inspire you, so choose something that uplifts your spirit every time you look at it

Week 12
The Quote Space

This week's goal is to add a quote to your workspace. Quotes can be reassuring, thought-provoking, and/or inspiring. A posted quote can remind us of our values, hopes, or interests, or even provide humor to our day. A quote can be a grounding statement that can help connect us to our work and/or our well-being.

OPTIONS

- A poster of a quote
- A printed or handwritten quote that you frame
- A small white or chalk board on which you can write a quote that you currently like
- A sticky note with your quote that you put inside a drawer or cabinet, for only you to see

CONSIDER EXPLORING

- Quotes from a favorite author or public figure
- Inspiration quotes that address the way you approach the world
- Humorous quotes that you might find on a coaster, bumper sticker, or t-shirt
- Something that someone has said to you recently that resonates

MAKE IT HAPPEN

- The key is that the quote is for you, so choose something that speaks to you.
- The size and public visibility of the quote can be modified based on need. An edgy, humorous quote can even be on a sticky note in the cabinet where you put/lock your bag for the day.
- Choose something that brings joy. No need to have something so aspirational that it actually makes you feel inadequate!

Remember: this is a fun quote for you, and it should evoke the type of response you need - if you need to be reminded of a daily thought or meditation, choose that, or if you need humor, by all means choose that

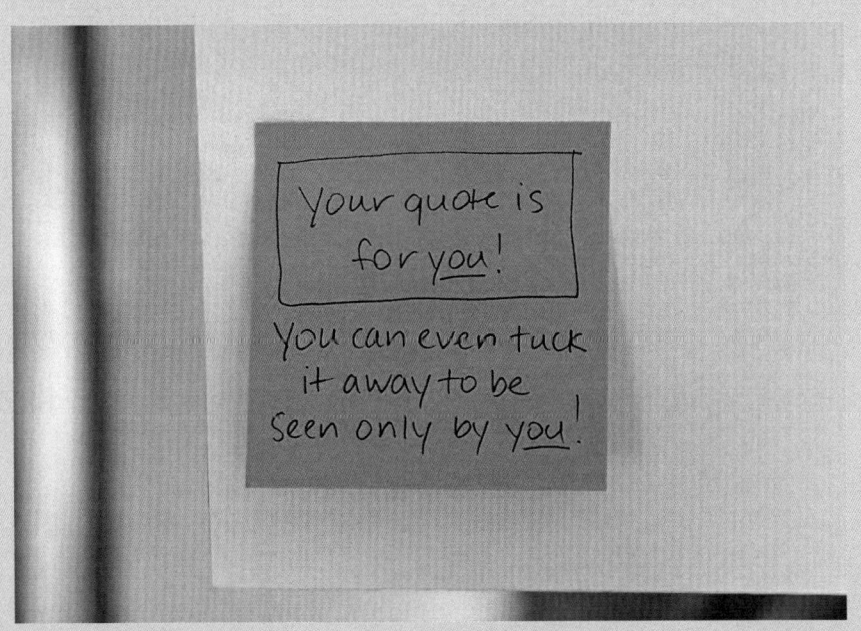

Week 13
The Lamp

The goal for this week is to add lighting to your workspace. Lighting can serve multiple functions. A desk lamp can provide focal light for paperwork tasks, or string lighting can provide a mood-improving glow to a space. Whether strictly functional or more ambiance-based, lighting can serve to lift your spirit. Also, a smaller lamp can give your eyes a break from overhead, full-room lights.

OPTIONS

- Desk-top lamp
- Clip-on or hanging lamp
- Floor lamp next to your desk area
- A string of lights draped in your desk area

ITEMS YOU CAN GATHER

- Lamp or string lights
- Bulb with preferred intensity and warmth
- Extension cord
- Batteries
- Command strips and/or hooks to attach string lights, etc.

MAKE IT HAPPEN

- If you are getting a lamp, personalize your choice by coordinating the color or texture of the lamp base and/or the shade with the colors you are using in your workspace.
- Choose bulbs that are consistent with your needs. Use bulbs appropriate for task lighting, ambiance, or both.
- Revisit cord management, if needed.

Remember: this light is for you to use during your preparation time, not necessarily when you are working with a room full of students, so choose it with yourself in mind

Week 14
The Walk

This week's goal is to take a daily walk to an outside space. Nature can calm and inspire our spirit. It may be that you could go for a full walk outside, or just step outside the door. You may be able to spare ten minutes, or even just two. With whatever time and space you have available, being able to connect with the outside will stimulate your senses and provide you a healthy moment of pause.

OPTIONS

- Stand outside an entry door
- Go for a walk outside your building
- Visit an interior, outdoor courtyard

IDEAS TO CONSIDER

- You could focus on looking at the sky and breathing in the fresh air.
- You could bring your drink and walk a bit or sit and enjoy your drink.
- A coworker might like to join you for your outside time.
- You could focus on the changes in nature you see each day.

MAKE IT HAPPEN

- It can be challenging to find a time to leave your room, but part of the idea is getting out of your room or your work office for a bit.
- If it is rainy or you have really limited options for accessing the outdoors, you could consider just being in a different space that has a window that you can open, when weather-appropriate.
- When you are out of your room to visit the restroom, you could consider getting outside for a moment before you head back to your room.

Remember: let the color, light, sound, and smells of nature refresh you, even if you can only enjoy them for a few minutes

Week 15
The Vase

Our focus this week is to set up a vase in your workspace. A vase allows for you to change what you display easily. Having seasonal foliage or flowers, or a special collection of items displayed, helps remind you of nature or special places or occasions. The vase can hold natural things that bring you joy.

OPTIONS

- A glass vase
- A mason jar, or other recycled jar
- A ceramic vase with or without decoration
- A pottery vase

ITEMS FOR YOUR VASE

- Stones, seaglass, or shells - if you can see into the vase
- Twigs
- Branches with greenery/leaves
- Flowers
- Leaves or grasses
- A collectible, such as pins or coins
- Something seasonal, such as bows or pine cones

MAKE IT HAPPEN

- Collect something as you go on your regular outdoors walk. Take scissors for a small, outdoor trimming.
- Try out a seasonal flower or greenery theme.
- Collect something in the vase over the year, such as road race numbers, ticket stubs, or programs, or something that reminds you of something you enjoy.

Remember: a see-through vase allows for opportunities to display collections, while a ceramic vase might be a great place have something from nature - you could even have one of each

Week 16
The Bowl

The goal of this week is to set up a beautiful bowl in a secure location. As teachers, we may need to take off and store a ring or stash a flashdrive, and a bowl in a drawer can provide an anchoring space to do that. Having the bowl be artistically and functionally appealing to you will make it an enjoyable space to secure your items.

OPTIONS

- Ceramic/pottery
- Wood
- Metal
- Glass
- Wicker

IDEAS TO CONSIDER

- Think of how it will function, and choose an appropriate size.
- Decide if you need something with a lid, and whether the lid needs to snap on or just sit on top of the bowl.
- Choose a color and material that goes with other choices you have made in previous weeks.

MAKE IT HAPPEN

- Think about if you need a spot for jewelry, hair ties, your keys, or reading glasses.
- Look through your desk drawer to see if you need to group anything into a bowl - maybe your paper clips are in the packaging box and you could move them to a nice container
- Maybe you need a beautiful bowl in your snack drawer, and you want to make an addition to that space.

Remember: the bowl is meant to be helpful in containing something, as well as appealing to you, so that it lifts your spirits when you see it

Week 17
The Screensaver

This week our goal will be to work on choosing a screensaver and/or a desktop wallpaper image. You look at your computer many times a day, but may not have a photo displayed in an intentional way. Seeing a familiar place, person, or pet can lift your day, or even connecting with some of the beautiful photography available for your desktop background can be grounding.

OPTIONS

- Your own photographs
- Images found online
- Options pre-stored in the computer

CONSIDER EXPLORING

- Photos of your family, pets, or garden
- Nature photography
- Photos from trips you have taken or places you want to go
- Artwork or designs that you love
- Simple color changes or geometric backgrounds
- A quote as part of the image

MAKE IT HAPPEN

- Go through your own camera roll to find photos that remind you of a connection or that make you feel happy or in awe of nature.
- Consider if you might like seasonal photos.
- Look online at downloads for either screensavers or desktop wallpaper.
- Consider creating a folder so that you have an anchor spot for images that you love so that you will have easy access when you want to make changes.

Remember: you are choosing some images or backgrounds consistent with your needs, so think about if you are looking for something calming or more vibrant

Week 18
The Organizer

The goal of this week is to bring a beautiful organizer into your space. You may have an older or less functional organizer, or you may see a need for a new, additional one. Pencil, paper, or desk drawer organizers can be more than utilitarian. They can be chosen based on the beauty of their natural material or color and thus serve to add both tidiness and beauty to your workspace.

OPTIONS

- Desk drawer organizer
- Paperwork holders
- Desk mat (blotter), mouse pad, coaster
- Wall organizer or peg board with attachments

IDEAS TO CONSIDER

- Pencil cup
- Something with compartments for paper clips, push pins, binder clips
- Drawer tray with spaces for pens and post-it notes
- Paper organizer in a beautiful color
- Trays or mats for grouping items

MAKE IT HAPPEN

- Choose a target area so that you are able to focus on both functionality and aesthetics.
- Assess your needs for that space. What would you like to group together, and how easily accessible would you like it to be?
- If you are using what you already have, take everything out and clean the space, and consider adding items of color into one section of the space.
- If you have larger items you want to organizes, mats, pads, and trays can work well for grouping.

Remember: as you either make an addition or exchange, think about how color, texture, and size will impact the space

Week 19
The Tools

This week you will be working to outfit yourself with basic household tools. On occasion we find ourselves in need of a screwdriver or tape measure, and it is valuable to go through whatever you have, and make adjustments to organize a great toolset. Having easy access to the tools you need helps build your confidence and feeling of preparedness to take care of your space.

OPTIONS

- An actual toolbox or tool bag
- A shoebox or other bin
- A section in a drawer with a few basic tools
- A single multi-tool

NEED TO GATHER

- Screwdriver
- Tape measure
- Adjustable wrench
- Pliers
- Hammer
- Duck tape
- Command strips

MAKE IT HAPPEN

- It is useful to have a Phillips and a flathead screwdriver. You can find screwdrivers with interchangeable tips to save space.
- You can add adhesives to your tool set such as command strips, tape, putty, or craft or epoxy glue.
- You could consider adding a few crafting-type items such as wire, a wirecutter, an exacto knife, or a paintbrush.

Remember: you don't need to go overboard, but just start with a few tools or adhesives, and group them together so that you have confidence that you have easy access to the items

Week 20
The Temperature

The goal this week is to evaluate and revise how you manage staying at a comfortable temperature. Schools often have heating systems that may not allow for much individual room control. It can be reassuring to have items to help you feel cooler or warmer.

OPTIONS

- Clothing
- Fan
- Water bottle

IDEAS TO CONSIDER

- Sweater
- Fleece
- Vest
- Jacket
- Scarf
- Window fan
- Small table-top fan
- Coat rack
- Hooks on a wall or door
- A cubby or drawer space

MAKE IT HAPPEN

- Ideally managing the temperature involves changing the control or opening windows.
- Keep a few clothing items for layering at school - choose a specific space to store them such as a cabinet or a freestanding or wall-based rack.
- For warmer months, consider getting a fan. Take the time to pursue getting one that can stay in your room or at your desk area.
- Cold water, as well as hot beverages, can also help with temperature management, so having a bottle or mug can be useful.

Remember: the key is to have a few items stored in a designated place, and as always, try to select colors and textures that bring you joy

Week 21
The Cushion

This week's goal involves adding some type of personal cushion to your space. Desk chairs and dress shoes can be uncomfortable. Cushions bring comfort to our backs, bottoms, and feet. It can be nice to have spaces in the day during which you have the physical support and comfort of a cushion.

OPTIONS

- Comfortable seating
- Propping your feet
- Cushioning your feet

ITEMS TO CONSIDER

- Seat pad or pillow for your desk chair
- An entirely new/different desk chair
- An ottoman
- A footstool
- A small rug under your desk area
- Slides
- Crocs/slippers

MAKE IT HAPPEN

- You could add a back support pillow or a pad to your desk chair to increase comfort.
- A small footstool would fit under your desk, and could be used while you grade or do paperwork.
- Adding a rug below your desk would allow you to slip off your shoes during your prep time and provide relief to your feet.
- Warm slippers or cushy slides could also be left below your desk, and you could slip them on during your planning time.

Remember: this is a small addition to provide yourself comfort - you may have alternative seating choices, etc, for your students, but this addition is exclusively for you

Week 22
The Idea Space

Our focus this week will be to create a space for making note of ideas. As we teach, we often think of things we'd like to try new or differently. Having an anchoring notebook space for your ideas gives you a centralized place for documenting creative ideas and notes.

OPTIONS

- Notebook
- Sticky notes or small loose-leaf paper
- Voice memos
- Space on your computer desktop

ITEMS YOU COULD GATHER

- A notebook or jotter
- A few beautiful pens or markers to be used with the notebook or other system
- Sticky notes
- Small loose-leaf paper or index cards and a box or jar that can hold them
- A voice memo system on your phone
- An ongoing document on your computer desktop, or a computer folder in which you save links

MAKE IT HAPPEN

- If you get a notebook, think about color, size, the weight of the paper, and whether you like spiral binding or not.
- Get the most exciting pens you can find. You are creatively gathering your ideas, so chose pens that inspire creative thinking.
- If a notebook is not appealing, you could consider using index cards, a small pad, or even scrap paper for writing down ideas. Then, keep a small box or jar nearby, and just put the ideas in the box whenever you need.

Remember: you want a system for keeping ideas that is very simple so that you can easily jot the ideas down and move on

Week 23
The Two Photos

Seeing photos of loved faces or places can help you feel connected during your day. They can help you remember positive experiences and reduce your stress. The goal this month will be to choose two photos and frames, and get them out in your workspace.

OPTIONS

- One of any version of nature that inspires you, outdoors or inside
- One of a special being, or a group of beings whom you love

IDEAS TO CONSIDER

- Outdoor scenes from trips
- Beach, mountain, or farm photos
- Favorite plants or a garden
- Family members
- Friends
- Pets
- Groups at a special event
- Activities that are hobbies
- You in a photo with others

MAKE IT HAPPEN

- Consider using nature photos from trips or places you love, as the photo will connect you to joyful memories.
- If you love gardening, fishing, or something outside, find a nature photo that connects with that activity.
- Choose a photo of a being that will make you smile.
- Think about frames that are slightly different in shape or size. Also think about combinations of pattern and plain, or matted and unmatted.

Remember: the photos are most important, but also find two frames that you feel look great together and go with the color choices you have made thus far for your space

Week 24
The Figurine

The goal this week is to create space for your whimsical figurines and/or magnets. These types of items foster happy energy or even humor. Having them in a grouping in your workspace, either more or less visible to all, can add joy to your day. If it is a small, fun decorative item, bring it on out this week.

OPTIONS

- Statues
- Action figures
- Creatures
- Rocks
- Magnets

ITEMS YOU CAN GATHER

- Bobble head
- Chia pet
- Lego figures
- Porcelain sculpture
- Crystal bird
- Snow globe
- Painted rock
- Tray for grouping items

MAKE IT HAPPEN

- You could display a single item or choose to have a small grouping that you set up on a decorative tray.
- The decorative items could match the seasons or holidays, be from a vacation, or be grouped with some other theme.
- It might be enjoyable to change out the display from time to time, as you might acquire new items you would like to rotate in.

Remember: whimsical figurines are meant to make you smile, so whether geeky, artsy, or frilly, enjoy your choices

Week 25
The Joy Box

Our last goal for our workspace will be to put together a joy box. Over the years, students, fellow teachers, parents, and others within your school may give you heartfelt notes of appreciation. Reading these notes on a rough day can help lift your spirit and remind you of the good work that you do. So for this final week, the last addition to your workspace will be to set up a beautiful container to keep these notes gathered together.

OPTIONS

- Wooden box
- Decorative box
- A shoebox that you decorate or wrap
- A basket with a lid
- A ceramic container with a lid
- A large envelope
- Decorative bag

CONSIDER EXPLORING

- Something that tucks into a drawer easily
- A container that would look nice on a shelf and is consistent with colors/textures you have chosen

MAKE IT HAPPEN

- Decide where you would like to store the container, so that you are able to narrow down the size and shape you would like best.
- Choose something that is easy to open and close and that is visually appealing on the outside.
- Find any notes or cards that you have gotten so far and add them to the container.
- If you are just starting out, you could even simply print out a nice email someone sent to start off your collection.

Remember: you chose this work because you wanted to help your students be excited about learning - let the words of others help keep you excited about being a teacher

WISHING YOU JOY

Striving to support young people as they learn and grow is a wonderful endeavor. As you gain experience as an educator, you will see that some trends in education are better than others. Schools can make overall programming choices that don't always support your own, individual, educational program that you offer students. Having a great workspace can't fix those challenges, but mindfully crafting your workspace is a way of taking stock in yourself. You are acknowledging and valuing your own needs.

Grow your support space for yourself as you would grow your curriculum. Engage with small changes that over time help bring you calm or make you smile, because you are working to take care of yourself. You have an identity that is separate from the groups of students you work with from year to year. Let some of your energy go to supporting that identity as you create a workspace that is just for you.

Made in United States
North Haven, CT
11 March 2024